Copyright @ 2020 John L. Godbolt

All rights reserved. No part of this book may be reproduced in any manner without written permission except in the case of brief quotations included in critical articles and reviews. For information, please contact the author.

Published in

Printed and Bound in the United States of America
ISBN:978-1-7340273-3-4

In Memory of Derrian J. Glenn
March 7, 1991 - April 6, 2020
"You lived your dash well!"

Dedication

This project is dedicated to the brave men and women who served our country; especially those who paid the ultimate price.

"You will never do anything in this world without courage. It is the greatest quality of the mind next to honor."

Aristotle

Introduction

Some of the best things in life happened by accident. For example, Penicillium, Corn Flakes, Teflon, Slinky, Silly Putty, Post-it-Notes, Popsicles, and the list goes on! People were attempting another feat and stumbled upon a better one! So it is with this Bible study project. My wife and I had all intentions of developing a self help guide that would accompany the series our church was studying - More Than a Conqueror. By accident, we embarked upon a more intense guide for every person seeking to understand and overcome personal challenges in their spiritual journey.

Romans 8:35 lists seven threats that are deadly and they seek to do permanent damage to the personal relationship between the child of God and his Lord and Savior, Jesus Christ. We took these threats seriously; we extensively and intricately looked at the influences they carry and how they operate against the believer. Then we suggested ways by which anyone practicing godly principles can overcome these threats.

Acknowledgments

Without a doubt, the skill set of Delarese Townsend and Helenea Dawson have proven, again, to be a gift to us in organizing this project. Ladies, we could not have done it without you! Your insight and attention to details added life and clarity to this work. Many thanks!

To my wife and strongest supporter, Vertell. Your time, energy and effort have been a guiding light over the many decades of our marriage and ministry. Thank you for being open and honest about this and all of the projects we have undertaken. I love you!

More Than Conquerors!

Bible Study Series

Romans 8:37- 39 - Nay, in all these things we are more than conquerors through him that loved us. 38 For I am persuaded, that neither death, nor life, nor angels, nor principalities, nor powers, nor things present, nor things to come, 39 Nor height, nor depth, nor any other creature, shall be able to separate us from the love of God, which is in Christ Jesus our Lord.

"What are the potential threats?"

In order to get a clear understanding of the scriptures in our text we need to research Romans 8:35, where the potential threats are listed.

Romans 8:35 - Who shall separate us from the love of Christ? shall tribulation, or distress, or persecution, or famine, or nakedness, or peril, or sword?

Verse 35 lists seven (7) potential threats to one's personal relationship with Christ. We must not allow pride to deceive us into thinking . . . "Not me! I got this!" This is one of the reasons the Holy Spirit inspired Paul to pen I Corinthians 9:27 - *But I keep under my body, and bring it into subjection: lest that by any means, when I have preached to others, I myself should be a castaway.*

Who can separate us?

The Greek word for *separation* is chorizo. It is so intimate in its nature that it is put in the context of a husband and wife divorcing. Not only is it a divorce, it is nasty. Chorizo means to put asunder, to go astray and to place room between. Not only is our separation from God compared to a divorce, it is considered a nasty break-up.

It is obvious that these seven threats are deadly and they seek to do permanent damage to the personal relationship between the child of God and his Lord and Savior, Jesus Christ. It is time to take these threats seriously and look at the influence they carry and how they operate against the believer.

1. Tribulation - in a word, tribulation is *pressure*! In the context of this scripture, it is a spirit of persuasion, influence or intimidation to make someone do something. Are you under pressure from your employment, family, finance, school, or any combination of these? If so, you need to confront these issues and prioritize your life with your spiritual man being first.
2. Distress - The Greek word is stenochoria, which means calamity, to narrow a place, and to face extreme affliction. Distress is a formidable foe. A good example of this is obsessively

following negative news reports, opinionated radio, and/or social media posts without having a positive outlet to combat the distressful spirit that accompanies these things. Jesus gives us the proper way to handle this kind of subtle attack. **Matthew 4:4 -But he answered and said, it is written, Man shall not live by bread alone, but by every word that proceedeth out the mouth of God.** Because we have a relationship with God through the Word of God, we have an antidote for distress.

3. Persecution - The essence of persecution is to make someone run or flee, or to drive them away. Persecution can be visible and invisible, tangible and intangible, audible and inaudible, and physical and mental.

4. Famine - The Greek word for famine is *li'-po*; a verb which means to leave, to fail or be absent: be destitute (wanting), and lack. Now, we can clearly see that this is not speaking of only natural food but any source of support lacking in one's life. A breakdown in parental, marital, social, or any other type of anticipated support that fails to meet our expectation can lead a person to a state of destitution. Feelings of loss, anger, and fear that stem from these types of breakdowns can be used by Satan against us in spiritual warfare. When we look back over our lives and see where other human beings have let us down, we must forgive and move forward! The natural tendencies are to question, blame and hold unforgiveness in our hearts. So, the

question is . . . will we allow this famine to separate (*cause a divorce*) from the love of Christ?

5. Nakedness - This word is *goom-not'-ace*, which is nudity. Think of it from the natural perspective of being in a church, school, or work setting and everyone has on the proper attire except you. Can you imagine the utter embarrassment and shame you would experience if this was your reality? Whether it has to do with the lack of education or training about something others possess and you do not, or being destitute due to poverty and having to endure the piercing eyes of those with the knowledge, resources and skills to provide for themselves, this question remains - will you allow it to separate

(*make you run away*) from the love of Christ?

6. Peril - The Greek word for peril is *kin'-doo-nos*, and it means danger. If anyone knows what it means to be in danger, it is the Apostle Paul. **II Corinthians 11:26 says - In journeyings often, in perils of waters, in perils of robbers, in perils by mine own countrymen, in perils by the heathen, in perils in the city, in perils in the wilderness, in perils in the sea, in perils among false brethren;** He specifically names eight (8) different perils: waters, robbers, countrymen, heathen, city, wilderness, sea, and false brethren.

    a. Waters - *Drinkable, fresh waters* should be considered safe, but this a warning to stay vigilant even when refreshing yourself.

b. *Robbers* - A robber is a blunder, one with an agenda to take or waste your valuables. Our greatest treasure is in the love of Christ!
c. *Countrymen* - These are *kindred, offspring*; spiritual children you may have birthed into the kingdom of God through prayer, fasting and teaching of the Word of God.
d. *Heathen* - These are *pagan people, or nations* with little or no understanding of your ministry assignment and could prove hostile to your intentions. Be aware!
e. *City* - Cities have walls, which are designed to protect. Paul had to be slid down over a wall in a basket because his life was

threatened by those who hated what he preached. Nevertheless, he did not allow that to stop his work.

f. *Wilderness* - This is a place of solitude or a desert. This is a picture of lonesomeness or a time of spiritual dryness. This is the time when Paul did not rethink his call but refocused his call. These are the times when our faith is tested because our labor may seem in vain. Never give up hope!

g. *Sea* - Acts 27: 27-38 details Paul's faithful fourteen days and nights journey on the dangerous seas. Even in these dangerous conditions he could encourage all 276 souls on board because he had the promise of God that he would preach again in Rome.

   h. *False Brethren* - The definition is *pretended associates*. Sadly, there are those who find it more appealing and satisfying to pretend than to contend for the faith. However discouraging that may be, we cannot allow it to interfere, hinder or stop our progress in Christ.

7. Sword - The Greek word is *makh'-ahee-rah*, which means a knife, dirk, figuratively war, or judicial punishment. When Paul speaks of this challenge to our spiritual journey, we can readily see that there are those who will get close enough to us to stab and cause a deep wound in our soul. This word means war and punishment. There are those who feel

justified, even called, to stop the teachings of the love of Christ. If nothing else, they will band together to attack every move you make. Never lose sight that it is not about you, but the Christ in you.

Study Questions:

1. What knowledge have you gained concerning the topic of potential threats?

_____
_____
_____
_____
_____
_____
_____
_____

Consider: Many Christians make a big mistake from the start by leaving out the people who may have experienced similar situations; consequently, they suffer alone and never hear solid testimonies and good suggestions that could help them. The people who are left out of the process suffer loss as well.

2. When you think of "*separate us*" as a divorce from Jesus, what do you see as a needful major step to organize your life choices in hopes of avoiding such a catastrophe?

_____
_____
_____
_____
_____
_____
_____
_____

Consider: If you aren't clear about where you want to go, you will not get there. You need a set of scripturally-based guiding principles with which you can align your life.

3. Where do your thoughts and feelings about *potential threats* stand as it relates to the real issue(s) in your life?

_____
_____
_____
_____
_____
_____
_____
_____

Consider: Too many Christians start to solve a problem or decide on a course of action before they understand the real issue(s). Understanding the real issue(s) pays off in the form of greater clarity and a deeper level of decision making.

4. Have you laid all the options out on the table? _____ .

Consider: It pays to lay out all challenges before making a decision. This discourages the tendency to settle on a course of action that could end in disaster.

5. What sources will you use to gather your information to combat *potential threats*?

_____

_____

_____

_____

_____

_____

_____

Consider: By working to gather information from several sources, you broaden your base and discourage the mistake of sticking to your personal viewpoint.

6. How do you plan to monitor whether your decisions are working and promptly modify

them as needed?

_____

_____

_____

_____

_____

_____

Consider: It is important to set a specific time frame in which to assess how well your plan is working. Be aware that situations change, and a good decision made previously may no longer be adequate for the current dilemma.

The Days of "Nay"

Romans 8:37 - *Nay, in all these things we are more than conquerors through him that loved us.*

"*Fix your mouth to say no!*" This is the advice I would hear as a child coming from the guardian adults in my life. Anytime I would put myself too far out on a limb to help, give too much money to a worthless cause, or give away something because I was too soft-hearted, I would hear that phrase piercing my eardrums. It took me years to finally understand that they could clearly see that others, with selfish intentions, picked up on my weaknesses. Even though the method was a bit crude and embarrassing, it finally sunk in . . . "*How long are you going to be a doormat* (not the original choice word) *and let people take advantage of your good nature? Learn how to say, no!* This is the same message we find in Romans 8:37.

Nay is Greek (allah) defined as nevertheless, notwithstanding, having an objection, exception or restriction to a particular matter.

The day that we begin to speak "Nay" to each and every negative thought, feeling, emotion and statement confronting us will be the beginning of the warrior standing up in us. We will be doing as Jesus did in the wilderness temptation – we will speak truth to power. Our wills are laid bare, and we are thrust into a place of major decision. We will speak the Word of God as did Jesus during His time of refining. Even though Jesus never used the word, nay, it is clearly implied throughout his confrontation with Satan. Each time Satan presented Jesus with a temptation, His reply was in opposition. In other words . . . No!

Matthew 4: 1 - Then was Jesus led up of the Spirit into the wilderness to be tempted of the devil.

When the Spirit of God leads us into a place of testing or discipline, it is for maturation and revelation. Warriors are not made because of someone's prophecies or mere laying on of hands. That is just the beginning. The true making comes when we, like Jesus, are brought to our personal wilderness experience, and we overcome them. This is where we are confronted with the three major temptations; lust of our flesh, the lust of our eyes and the pride of life. **I John 2:16 - For all that is in the world, the lust of the flesh, and the lust of the eyes, and the pride of life, is not of the Father, but is of the world.**

Matthew 4: 2 And when he had fasted forty days and forty nights, he was afterward an hungered.

The Greek word for hungered means to be famished. Jesus' appetite for food was at an all time high. In other words, He was at His weakest and most vulnerable state for being tempted to eat, and to succumb to Satan's temptation. Based on our level of experience in Christ and our familiarity with His Word, we too, can be tested at our weakest and most vulnerable moment. Yet, just like Jesus, we can stand the wicked onslaught of Satan.

Matthew 4: 3 And when the tempter came to him, he said, If thou be the Son of God, command that these stones be made bread. Matthew uses the word, tempter, which means *endeavor, scrutinize, entice, examine, to go about and to prove.* I have a relative and fellow Christian pastor in the Gospel of Jesus Christ, who is skilled in furniture restoration. One day, I was in his shop admiring a beautiful piece of furniture. He explained the process that it took to get the texture and the vibrant sheen to make it stand out. I could see a great correlation in the way God develops His overcoming Christians as he explained the process.

1. The Stripping Process - This is where the old, dilapidated and tarnished material was removed. The wood has to be brought back to its original state. *No matter the amount of carnality, the number of wounds or the abuse we have endured, the Blood of Jesus and the Waters of His Great Name are available to remove the stain of sin*

2. The Repairing Process - Because paint can cover up damaged areas, there has to be a repairing process where a wood base product is used to bond with the piece of furniture. **Hebrews 4:15 - For we have not an high priest**

which cannot be touched with the feeling of our infirmities; but was in all points tempted like as we are, yet without sin. In order for us to be totally repaired, we must bond with the finished word of Calvary and the "wood" He was crucified upon. He knows our pain, guilt and sufferings and He has already paid the price.

3. The Healing Process - Because the process could have caused stress (yes, stress!) on the wood, it is given time and space to recover (dry) and bond with the product. **Matthew 11:28 - Come unto me, all ye that labour and are heavy laden, and I will give you rest.** Rest is Greek (an-ap-ow'-o) which means to repose, be exempt, remain, take ease, and refresh. It is so reassuring that God does not hold our past over our heads and make us pay

restitution or suffer the full force of the consequences. He gives us space and time to heal.

4. The Sanding Process - The severity of this stage is directly aligned with the amount of damage to the wood, and the purpose for the piece of furniture. Thus, the grit grade of the sandpaper used in this stage is important. For heavy sanding and stripping, he needed coarse sandpaper measuring 40- to 60-grit; for smoothing surfaces and removing small imperfections, he would choose 80- to 120-grit sandpaper. And for finishing surfaces smoothly, he would use a super fine sandpaper with 360- to 600-grit. There are grit grades all the way to 1200! *Deep wounds may be a sign of the call and ministry in your life. Paul was a menace to the church before his*

conversion. He used every means necessary to bring Christians back to their original belief or worse! Once he accepted Jesus as Lord and Christ, he went to Peter for his ordination and commission. He had a great deal to do, so he had to get the Apostles to lay hands on him. So it is with us. The deeper the wound in our lives, the greater the application of the Blood, Word and Fire (sandpaper) needed to be applied to our situation.

5. The Staining Process - The whole objective for staining is to penetrate the wood. This process wards off any possible flaws in the final stages of the process. (**Hebrews 12:1 Wherefore seeing we also are compassed about with so great a cloud of witnesses, let us lay aside every weight, and the sin which doth so easily beset us, and let**

us run with patience the race that is set before us, . . .) God knows and understands our weakness and frailties, so He gives us His Word to apply layer after layer onto the deep wounds in our lives. These wounds may be past involvements that could return in some other form. Speaking the Word, worshiping and showing gratitude for God's provision allows the process of redemption to go deep into the soul of the believer.

6. The Waiting Period - The furniture has to be laid aside for a period of time to bond, heal, and strengthen for the next three (3) or four (4) stages. Too often, we want to jump into our ministry gifts and begin working for the Lord. However, a season of rest is a great place to learn the true intentions of our heart. I have seen people with

great potential skip this season, only to end up worse in the end than their beginning stage. Pride and shame sets in and they become hyper-spiritual and/or accusatory. Instead of humbling themselves, repenting and returning to the starting point, they push past their conscience to impress the world with their gift. Now they are operating God's gift for their personal glory. God will not bless a mess!

7. The Sealing Process - Sometimes, there are surfaces and those slightly below the surface that have nicks, nail holes, or something that splinters the surface. The restorer uses a product called wood filler that can fill in the holes and bond to the surface of the wood furniture. *When we go into worship, God's Holy Spirit searches our heart and finds those nicks and*

splintered places that were left from the past. Like a dove brooding over the nest, Holy Spirit covers us over and works on the hidden and surface areas of our life. God's plan is perfect!

8. The Spraying Process - Only a trained professional can match the "oil" with the natural coloring of the wood. Depending on the pigmentation of the wood, this process could take several rounds. *God is perfect at matching our gifts and callings with our assignment. Never assume you know this. Many times, it starts out in one place and shifts to another. There are promotions in God, too!*

9. The Finishing Process - Once the wood is brought back to its natural color, it must endure the finishing paper. The finishing paper is not as coarse as the sandpaper but works in

a similar manner. The difference is that the finishing paper is used to bring the sheen out in the wood. The more sheen desired the finer the finishing grade of the paper. *God's ways of aligning us with accountability partners, mentors and leaders only help to bring out the glow He wants His children to have. This process cannot happen if you are determined to be a "rogue" saint. We need each other to get through this final stage.*

Verse 4. But he answered and said, It is written, Man shall not live by bread alone, but by every word that proceedeth out of the mouth of God.
Satan is predictable. He always tempts us with the obvious. It was obvious Jesus was hungry after forty (40) days of fasting, so Satan does not bring him any food but

tempts Jesus to bring it forth of His own will. In other words, do a necessary thing, but out of your own strength. The revelation we can gain from a similar wilderness experience is the view at the strength of our carnal nature and the power of the Word to contain it. Even with a gnawing pain in the pit of His stomach, Jesus was composed and resigned to do God's Will.

Matthew 4: 5 - 7 Then the devil taketh him up into the holy city, and setteth him on a pinnacle of the temple, And saith unto him, If thou be the Son of God, cast thyself down: for it is written, He shall give his angels charge concerning thee: and in their hands they shall bear thee up, lest at any time thou dash thy foot against a stone. Jesus said unto him, It is written again, Thou shalt not tempt the Lord thy God.

Jesus used a different word for "Thou shalt not *tempt* the Lord thy God" than the word we see in verse 1 (to be *tempted* of the devil). This word is ekpeirazō, which means to do something out of place, time or cause. Jesus cut Satan sharply with this Word because that is exactly what Satan did. He misquoted a portion of Psalm 91 and used it totally out of context. When you read Psalm 91, you will clearly see that this portion of scripture speaks of God sending His angels to keep His children from harm of evil and plagues.

> **Psalm 91:10 -12 There shall no evil befall thee, neither shall any plague come nigh thy dwelling. For he shall give his angels charge over thee, to keep thee in all thy ways. They shall bear thee up in their hands, lest thou dash thy foot against a stone.**

Satan conveniently started in the middle of a thought to take the scripture out of context.

Jesus quoted from Deuteronomy 6:16 - *Ye shall not tempt the LORD your God, as ye tempted him in Massah.*

Matthew 4:8 - 10 Again, the devil taketh him up into an exceeding high mountain, and showeth him all the kingdoms of the world, and the glory of them; And saith unto him, All these things will I give thee, if thou wilt fall down and worship me. Then saith Jesus unto him, Get thee hence, Satan: for it is written, Thou shalt worship the Lord thy God, and him only shalt thou serve.

The first temptation was the lust of the flesh. Jesus overcame personal fleshly desires to gain spiritual growth. The second temptation was the lust of the eyes. Jesus overcame Satan's test to prove Himself in the eyes of creation. It is most important for us to be trusted with these gifts and talents for the glory of God and the salvation of mankind.

Our gifts and talents are tools for the Kingdom of God, not toys for entertainment of men. The third temptation was the pride of life. Jesus overcame the temptation of power and influence. It is a well known fact that power and influence can get us into high places with man. Letting down the standard of holiness is not considered a major concern in this society. The world uses the term "The end justifies the means." In layman's term . . . you are not judged by the method you use but by the end results. If the use of power and influence acquires the desired goal, society says, *"it doesn't matter what method you use."* That is not acceptable to those of us who live by God's standard of character and holiness. **Philippians 4:8 - Finally, brethren, whatsoever things are true, whatsoever things are honest, whatsoever things are just, whatsoever things are pure, whatsoever things are lovely, whatsoever** *things are of a good report; if there be any virtue, and if there be any praise, think on these things.*

Matthew 4:11. Then the devil leaveth him, and, behold, angels came and ministered unto him.

Yes, there is a season when Satan will leave you and God uses His angels, some visible and some invisible, to minister natural and spiritual food to you. God allows us a season of refreshing and rebuilding. We are not always under great pressure and ridicule. There are times of rest and recuperation.

Study Questions:
1. What is the definition of Nay?

   _____
   _____
   _____
   _____
   _____
   _____

   Consider: One of the difficult words to say is "No!" Many people will give you a passive "no" by not showing up or not returning a call, text or even making eye contact. The fear of causing conflict is one of the major components in this equation. Ask yourself these questions...When and with whom are you not a people-pleaser? What do you believe will happen if you say "no"?

2. Why does the Spirit of God lead us into a place of testing?

   _____
   _____
   _____
   _____
   _____
   _____

_____
_____

Consider: Testing and temptation are not synonymous. Matthew 6:13 teaches us to pray . . . "**lead us not into temptation.**" Temptations are tools that lead us into ungodly influences. Testings are trials which leads us into a deeper relationship with Jesus, a greater appreciation of His Word and a greater understanding of His purpose.

3. What is the purpose of Jesus saying . . . "**It is written**" in the wilderness?
_____
_____
_____
_____
_____
_____
_____
_____

Consider: Dr. John Piper's article on "Why Memorize Scripture?" gives six (6) reasons for putting the Word of God to memory:

    1. Bible memorization has the effect of making our gaze on Jesus steadier and clearer.
    2. It is the power to slay the temptation to sin.
    3. Daily scripture quotation puts Satan to flight.
    4. The Word of God is a comfort and counsel to those we love.
    5. Quoting the scripture is an effective communication to unbelievers.
    6. It is the way to commune with God.

4. What is the definition of "tempter," and how would you describe your response to temptation?

_____
_____
_____
_____
_____
_____
_____
____

5. Why was Satan attempting to get Christ to worship him, and how does he tempt you to do the same?

   _____
   _____
   _____
   _____
   _____
   _____
   _____
   _____

   Consider: The act of committing a mortal sin destroys the moral fiber of the believer. In and of itself, committing a mortal sin is a rejection of God. If left un-reconciled, mortal sins will lead to eternal separation from God.

Types of Strongholds

Since our focus is concentrated on inward warfare, we must look at strongholds as areas of darkness within the mind or personality that causes ongoing spiritual or emotional behavioral problems. Let's look at twelve (12) specific types of strongholds and the behaviors produced by each.

1. BITTERNESS
    a. Resentment - bitter indignation at having been treated unfairly
    b. Hate - intense feelings or passionate dislike for (someone)
    c. Unforgiveness - unwilling or unable to forgive
    d. Anger - displeasure, or hostility
    e. Violence - behavior involving physical force intended to hurt or kill
    f. Revenge - the action of inflicting hurt or harm on someone

2. HEAVINESS
    a. Depression - a state of general unhappiness or despondency
    b. Despair - complete loss or absence of hope

c. Self-pity - excessive, self-absorbed unhappiness over one's own troubles
   d. Loneliness - sadness
   e. Addictions - physically and mentally dependent on a particular substance
   f. Suicide - the action of killing oneself intentionally

3. INSECURITY
   a. Inferiority - having a sense of imperfection or poorness when compared to others
   b. Inadequacy - lacking the quantity or quality required
   c. Timidity - lacking courage or confidence
   d. Shyness/Withdrawal - lacking courage or confidence
   e. Pleasing people, not God - working to satisfy or appeal to people instead of God
   f. Lack of trust/worry - giving way to anxiety or uneasiness
   g. Wrong relationships - connecting too deeply with the wrong people

4. CONTROL

a. Manipulation - the act of deceiving someone in a clever or unscrupulous way
   b. Striving - making great efforts to achieve or obtain something
   c. Lack of trust - a feeling that someone or something is not honest and cannot be trusted
   d. Worry - giving way to anxiety or uneasiness
   e. Insensitivity - lack of concern for others' feelings
   f. Desire for recognition - acknowledgment of something's existence, validity, or legality

5. JEALOUSY
   a. Spitefulness - showing or causing malice
   b. Gossip/slander - conversations about others involving details that are not confirmed as being true
   c. Betrayal - being disloyal
   d. Critical spirit - expressing disapproving comments or judgments
   e. Judgmental - making decisions or conclusions without sound evidence
   f. Suspicious nature - distrustful without a cause

6. IDOLATRY
   a. Frustration - the feeling of being upset or annoyed
   b. Hopelessness - the feeling or state of despair
   c. Selfishness/Greed - intense and selfish desire for something
   d. Financial problems - making unsound decisions with money
   e. Wrong goals/Decisions - putting ambition and effort in unfruitful projects
   f. Confusion/Living a lie - one's fantasy is not factual or consistent with reality
   g. Pursuing dead ends - putting effort into dreams, plans and goals with no tangible reward
   h. Spiritual blindness/Apathy - lack of interest or knowledge in godly things
   i. Distractions - unable to give full attention to the things that truly matter

7. REBELLION
   a. Self Will - doing what pleases self
   b. Stubbornness - determined not to be changed

c. Strife - angry or bitter disagreements
   d. Factions - a small organized dissenting group
   e. Divisions - actions and behaviors causing separation
   f. Anger/Arguments - having a diverse view and expressing it in harsh tones
   g. Independent spirit - determined to stay free from other's authority
   h. Unteachable - unwillingness to learn
8. PRIDE
   a. Vanity - excessive pride in or admiration of one's own appearance or achievements.
   b. Self-righteousness - a state of being smug, hypocrisy, self-satisfaction
   c. Self-centered - preoccupied with oneself or affairs
   d. Insensitivity - lack of concern for others' feelings
   e. Materialism - a tendency to consider material possessions and physical comfort as more important than spiritual values
   f. Unteachable - unwillingness to learn

    g. Seeks positions - an attempt to use others to gain a higher or more important status

9. SEXUAL IMPURITY
   a. Lust - extremely strong sexual desire
   b. Seductiveness - tempting and attractive; enticing
   c. Masturbation - stimulation of the genitals with the hand for sexual pleasure
   d. Fornication - sexual intercourse between people not married to each other
   e. Adultery - voluntary sexual intercourse between a married person and a person who is not his or her spouse
   f. Frigidity - Failure of a male or female to respond to sexual stimulus
   g. Homosexuality - the quality or characteristic of being sexually attracted solely to people of one's own sex
   h. Pornography - printed or visual material containing the explicit description or display of sexual organs or activity

10. REJECTION

a. Addictions - being mentally and physically dependent on a particular substance, thing, or activity
   b. Compulsions - an irresistible urge to behave in a certain way
   c. Seeking acceptance - the action or process of being received as adequate or suitable
   d. Unworthiness -not deserving effort, attention, or respect
   e. Withdrawal - the action of discontinuing, removing, or terminating something

11. DECEIT
    a. Lying - not telling the whole truth
    b. Fantasies - the faculty or activity of imagining things, especially things that are impossible or improbable
    c. Delusions - an idiosyncratic belief or impression that is firmly maintained despite being contradicted by what is generally accepted as reality or rational argument
    d. Rationalizing - attempt to explain or justify (one's own or another's behavior or attitude) with logical, plausible reasons,

even if these are not true or appropriate
  e. Wrong (False) Doctrine - an untrue belief or set of beliefs held and taught as correct
  f. Misuse of Scripture - use of the Word of God in the wrong way or for the wrong purpose

12. FEAR
  a. Phobias - an extreme or irrational fear of or aversion to something
  b. Compulsions - an irresistible urge to behave in a certain way
  c. Perfectionism - refusal to accept any standard short of perfection
  d. Failure - lack of success
  e. Inability to set goals - unable to set or reach a desired ambition

Study Questions:
1. Being totally honest with yourself, which of these areas do you find your greatest struggle and why?

   _____
   _____
   _____
   _____
   _____
   _____
   _____
   _____
   _____
   _____
   _____

2. When did you first notice this behavior in your life, and what did you do about it?

   _____
   _____

_____

_____

_____

_____

_____

_____

3. Have you sought help to overcome this behavior, and what were the results?

_____

_____

_____

_____

_____

_____

_____

_____

Defeating Strongholds

A stronghold can be anything from an undisclosed habit that has gotten out of control to a generational issue that plagues the entire family. In either case, the Christian(s) in the home must take swift and decisive actions against it. The sooner, the better! Here are some steps to help tear down these strongholds in the Name of Jesus!

For The Natural Man:

1. Have such a personal relationship that you know the voice of God without any doubt.
2. Seek out other committed servants of God, who have overcome similar struggles and make them your accountability partners.
3. Get in the best physical shape possible. Warfare in the Spirit, like

natural warfare is mentally and physically taxing.
4. Pay off all of your debts! You are so much freer and able to focus on others when your life is in order.
5. Take a real vacation. Leave the job and work behind so you can relax and recuperate.

For The Spiritual Man:
1. BE HONEST

    Psalm 32:5 I acknowledged my sin unto thee, and mine iniquity have I not hid. I said, I will confess my transgressions unto the LORD; and thou forgavest the iniquity of my sin. Too many Christians are living double standards. They have secrets. So, they operate out of their gifts, but their personal life needs major repair. The good news is that we can get help by allowing the Blood of Jesus to penetrate our souls and the Word and the Spirit to work on us!

2. WALK IN HUMILITY
Humility is the recognition that you are dependent upon God and His provision for deliverance. *James 4:6,7 - But he giveth more grace. Wherefore he saith, God resisteth the proud, but giveth grace unto the humble.*
7. Submit yourselves therefore to God. Resist the devil, and he will flee from you.

3. BE QUICK TO REPENT (Even if you are not the guilty party)
Repentance is a determined, deliberate turning away from sin and the works of Satan.
Acts 2:38 Then Peter said unto them, Repent, and be baptized every one of you in the name of Jesus Christ for the

remission of sins, and ye shall receive the gift of the Holy Ghost.

4. RENUNCIATION

    Renunciation is the forsaking of evil. It is an action resulting from repentance. Remember, you cannot rebuke, cast out or cast down a spirit in someone else or in the atmosphere, if there is a lustful desire or spirit of pity for it inside of you. **Acts 19:18-19 And many that believed came, and confessed, and shewed their deeds. 19 Many of them also which used curious arts brought their books together, and burned them before all men: and they counted the price of them, and found it fifty thousand pieces of silver.**

5. BE QUICK TO FORGIVE

    God freely forgives all who confess their sins (1John 1:9), and we must also forgive others who have wronged us. Forgiveness is essential to deliverance.

Matthew 6:14-15 *For if ye forgive men their trespasses, your heavenly Father will also forgive you: 15 But if ye forgive not men their trespasses, neither will your Father forgive your trespasses.*

6. STEP UP IN YOUR PRAYER LIFE

    Ask God to deliver you and set you completely free.

    Joel 2:32 and it shall come to pass, that whosoever shall call on the name of the Lord shall be delivered: for in mount Zion and in Jerusalem shall be deliverance, as the Lord hath said, and in the remnant whom the Lord shall call.

7. REMEMBER THAT YOU ARE IN A WARFARE

Our warfare prayer is against demonic principalities and powers. It's not flesh but spiritual. **Ephesians 6:12 - For we wrestle not against flesh and blood, but against principalities, against powers, against the rulers of the darkness of this world, against spiritual wickedness in high places.**

8. USE THE WORD OF GOD

   In order to overcome this type of warfare, we must speak the Word of God when praying, worshipping, and fellowshipping. **Psalm 107:20 - He sent his word, and healed them, and delivered them from their destructions.**

Study Questions:
1. Where do you see weaknesses in the proper use of your spiritual resources?

   _____
   _____
   _____
   _____
   _____
   _____
   _____
   _____

2. Why do you think "being honest" is so high on the list?

   _____
   _____
   _____
   _____
   _____
   _____

3. How does having a healthy financial portfolio help in the life of others?

4. What is repentance, and how does it work?

The Posture of an Overcomer: A Demeanor of Determination!

Romans 8: 38, 39 - For I am persuaded, that neither death, nor life, nor angels, nor principalities, nor powers, nor things present, nor things to come,

39 Nor height, nor depth, nor any other creature, shall be able to separate us from the love of God, which is in Christ Jesus our Lord.

The definition of persuaded *is to trust, have confidence, to be confident, to listen, and to induce one to persuasion.*

I call this *spiritual swagger*! It means having the spiritual posture of a committed believer that can be seen from afar. To further explain, when we have our trust in God's Word and we have laid our thoughts, emotions, and plans at His Feet, we can rest in confidence that we are in the best of care. Since the first stage of overcoming is within, then it stands to reason that our demeanor or posture against any outward temptation would not falter under pressure. Jesus is our perfect example.

The Posture of Jesus

Matthew 27:12-14 And when he was accused of the chief priests and elders, he answered nothing. 13. Then said Pilate unto him, Hearest thou not how many things they witness against thee? 14. And he answered him to never a word; insomuch that the governor marvelled greatly.

The Son of God held up under every type of temptation during His mock trial, scourging by the Roman soldiers, journey to Calvary, and while being crucified under the cruel jeers of the crowd. Jesus endured it all! That same Blood and Spiritual constitution is available for each of us. All we need to do is trade our words for His Word; our will for

His Will; our way for His Way and our plans for His Plans!

The Posture of Peter

Acts 2:13-16 - 13. Others mocking said, These men are full of new wine. 14. But Peter, standing up with the eleven, lifted up his voice, and said unto them, Ye men of Judaea, and all ye that dwell at Jerusalem, be this known unto you, and hearken to my words: 15. For these are not drunken, as ye suppose, seeing it is but the third hour of the day. 16. But this is that which was spoken by the prophet Joel;

This is not the same Peter who denied Jesus three times before His Crucifixion. No, this Peter is filled with the Holy Ghost and is boldly proclaiming Jesus as Savior and what the Word of God has to say about his current condition. This is why it is vital for each born again believer in Jesus Christ to have the baptism of the Holy Ghost and Fire (Luke 3:16). The Holy Ghost is God's gift to us that reshapes our spiritual man, gives us understanding of His Word and makes us bold spokespersons for the gospel of Jesus Christ!

The Posture of Paul

Philippians 4:11- 13 - [11]Not that I speak in respect of want: for I have learned, in whatsoever state I am, therewith to be content. [12]I know both how to be abased, and I know how to abound: every where and in all things I am instructed both to be full and to be hungry, both to abound and to suffer need. [13]I can do all things through Christ which strengtheneth me. Ironically, the physical stature of Paul was short compared to the average height of the men in his day. However, none stood taller than Paul when it came to the teaching and preaching of The

Word of God. Paul's spiritual posture was steadfast through shipwrecks, beatings, attempts of murder on his life, hunger, sicknesses, rejections, overcoming false brethren, snake bites and the list goes on. On one side of the scales, his journey is different because he was tasked with introducing the gospel of Jesus Christ to the Gentile world. Yet, we have a world in which we travel in our everyday lives: however, in this world there are many who do not know Jesus. We need the posture of Apostle Paul to share Jesus with the lost souls in our world.

Study Questions:
1. Why is it impossible to fake spiritual posture?

   _____
   _____
   _____
   _____
   _____
   _____
   _____
   _____

2. How does one build his/her confidence in the Word of God?

   _____
   _____
   _____
   _____
   _____
   _____
   _____
   _____

3. Why does God give us His Word and examples of other overcomers?

   _____
   _____
   _____
   _____
   _____
   _____
   _____
   _____

4. What are some ways you can build your *spiritual swagger*?

   _____
   _____
   _____
   _____
   _____
   _____
   _____
   _____

We sincerely hope that our goal to inspire you to look deeply into your heart and work closely with the Holy Spirit to reveal hidden issues and sharpen your skills in spiritual warfare was accomplished. God has provided us with His divine plan to deliver us from all evil. We must stay humble and seek Him for life. (Proverbs 4:23)

May God's riches and best be yours!

John & Vertell

www.ingramcontent.com/pod-product-compliance
Lightning Source LLC
Chambersburg PA
CBHW041305110426
42743CB00037B/5